THE MODERN NERD'S GUIDE TO
LARPing

BY MICHAEL E. SCIANDRA

Gareth Stevens
PUBLISHING

Please visit our website, www.garethstevens.com. For a free color catalog of all our high-quality books, call toll free 1-800-542-2595 or fax 1-877-542-2596.

Cataloging-in-Publication Data

Names: Sciandra, Michael E.
Title: The modern nerd's guide to LARPing / Michael E. Sciandra.
Description: New York : Gareth Stevens Publishing, 2018. | Series: Geek out! | Includes index.
Identifiers: ISBN 9781538212097 (pbk.) | ISBN 9781538212110 (library bound) | ISBN 9781538212103 (6 pack)
Subjects: LCSH: Fantasy games–Juvenile literature. | Adventure games–Juvenile literature. | Role playing–Juvenile literature.
Classification: LCC GV1469.6 S35 2018 | DDC 793.93–dc23

First Edition

Published in 2018 by
Gareth Stevens Publishing
111 East 14th Street, Suite 349
New York, NY 10003

Copyright © 2018 Gareth Stevens Publishing

Designer: Sarah Liddell
Editor: Joan Stoltman

Photo credits: Cover, pp. 1, 4, 17 RalfHuels/Wikimedia Commons; texture used throughout StrelaStudio/Shutterstock.com; p. 5 Irve/Wikimedia Commons; p. 6 Blackregis/Shutterstock.com; p. 7 oTaToRo/Shutterstock.com; p. 8 Avivi Aharon/Shutterstock.com; p. 9 merzzie/Shutterstock.com; p. 13 Candela Foto Art/Kreuziger/The Image Bank/Getty Images; pp. 15, 19, 25 photos courtesy of Liz Paulie; pp. 18, 22 MLADEN ANTONOV/Staff/AFP/Getty Images; p. 21 AdmiralHood/Wikimedia Commons; p. 23 Tereshchenko Dmitry/Shutterstock.com; p. 27 SmilingHotel/Shutterstock.com; p. 29 photo courtesy of Allison Kern.

Printed in the United States of America

CPSIA compliance information: Batch #CW18GS: For further information contact Gareth Stevens, New York, New York at 1-800-542-2595.

CONTENTS

Words in the glossary appear in **bold** type the first time they are used in the text.

HEARD OF IT?

Chances are you've heard of LARPing before. But did you know that LARP stands for live action role-playing? "Live action" means that the action and **conversation** wasn't written out or even decided ahead of time. People create the stories as they go. Anything can happen!

Role-playing is a lot like being an actor or actress in a movie. When performers act like a character, that's role-playing or "being in character." Role-playing includes trying to sound, walk, dress, and act just like the character might if they were real. Inspiration for how a character might act can come from movies, TV, books, or real life!

Adventurers like these would be right at home in a **fantasy** LARP. But there are many other types of LARPs, too!

ALL KINDS OF LARPS

There are many groups and societies dedicated to LARPing. Usually, they each center on a certain theme. For example, a company called Rule of 3 Productions runs popular **science fiction**, or sci-fi, LARPs in Georgia that let you be a member of different tribal or human races!

THE STORY OF LARP

You may think LARP is new, but it's actually been around for decades! Role-playing games (RPGs) have been around even longer. Many LARPs are based on tabletop RPGs, often just called card and board games. But some parts of LARP go back to practices in Europe hundreds of years ago.

In both LARP and RPGs, each player has a character. In an RPG, each person plays their character using cards or pieces on a board. There's often an end goal in mind that characters are moving toward. LARPing, on the other hand, is trying to make the imagined story and setting a real experience through costumes and **props**.

In D&D, players roll a 20-sided die to decide different actions and moves. A 20-sided die is also an important part of play in Magic: The Gathering and other RPGs.

DUNGEONS AND DRAGONS

The most popular tabletop RPG ever is Dungeons and Dragons (D&D). A player called the dungeon master creates detailed stories ahead of time. Then the other players play as characters within these stories. Each character has the power to affect where the story goes, so everyone creates the experience together!

WHAT THEME INTERESTS YOU?

➤ Many people think LARPs only do fantasy themes. While fantasy is a big part of LARP's origin, it's only one of the many kinds of LARPs out there to enjoy! Science fiction is a common theme in LARP. Even history has a role in LARPing today!

The Mind's Eye Society creates LARP events using three tabletop games set in the fictional, or make-believe, World of Darkness. Other LARPs let you play in well-known imaginary worlds, such as the Marvel Comics universe. Inspired by the Harry Potter book series, the New World Magischola LARP lets players attend a fictional school to become a witch or **wizard**! What theme interests you?

Since LARPs always want new players, their websites will also tell you where and when LARP events will be held.

FINDING A LARP

Most LARPs have a website where anyone who's interested can read the story and rules of the LARP. Players also use these websites to talk to each other about future events, share pictures of past events, and discuss tips on making props and costumes. For every LARP, there's an online community!

CHOOSING YOUR LARP

Once you know what theme you're interested in, choosing which LARP to attend is about knowing what kind of action you're looking for. If you don't like weapons and fighting, you'd want to choose a LARP with limited battle role-play, like a no-touch, light-touch, theater-style, or no-combat LARP. Some battle LARPs allow people to play as noncombatant characters (NCCs), or characters that don't fight during battle!

No matter who you are, where you come from, or what your situation is, the people who run the LARP—called storytellers (STs)—work hard to make sure everybody has fun, feels welcome, and doesn't feel judged!

AGE LIMITS

When deciding which LARP to go to, read the rules first to make sure you can **participate** before making costumes and props. Many LARPs only allow people over 18. Some allow anyone under 13 with approval from their parents. But don't worry. There are LARPs out there for all ages!

AGE OF LARP PARTICIPANTS IN THE UNITED STATES

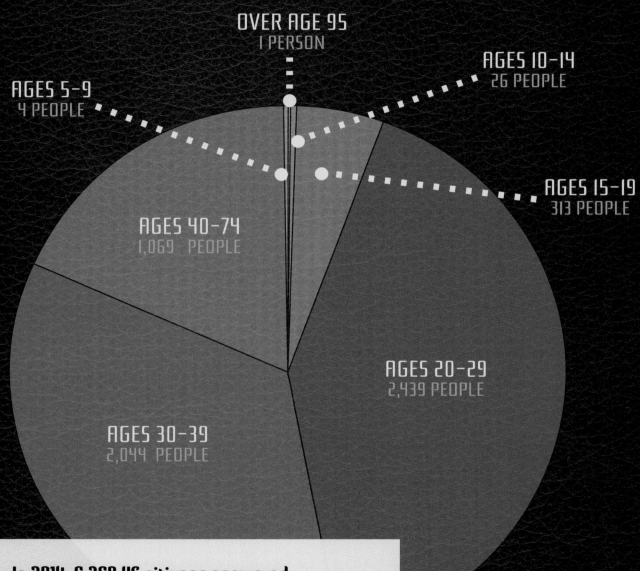

OVER AGE 95
1 PERSON

AGES 10-14
26 PEOPLE

AGES 5-9
4 PEOPLE

AGES 15-19
313 PEOPLE

AGES 40-74
1,069 PEOPLE

AGES 20-29
2,439 PEOPLE

AGES 30-39
2,044 PEOPLE

In 2014, 6,260 US citizens answered questions about how they LARPed. Though 364 didn't give an age, the largest group of people were in their 20s.

TIME TO STUDY!

Once you've chosen a LARP, it's important to learn everything you can about its universe! Some LARPers say that diving into the world of your LARP for the first time is one of the best parts of LARPing—other than actually playing, of course!

Whether it's on a website or in a book, be sure to read as much as you can about your LARP. The rules are especially important to read. Also, LARP worlds often have a history you'll want to know to play the game better. The STs have decided many details for the LARP, and the more you know, the more fun it is to play!

THE EVENT

LARP events are also called LARPs. Some LARPs only run once ever, others require a new character every time you play. Some LARPs have multiple stories that get played for a certain number of events. Knowing what kind of event you're at can change how you play!

In LARP, you help decide where the story goes within the rules of the LARP. If you and a friend are **pirates**, you may even choose to overthrow your ship's captain!

CREATING A CHARACTER

For both LARPs and RPGs, the work you do to create your character will all happen before getting together with other people to play. This work takes place at home and could take hours or months. This all depends on how many features you want in your character!

LARP and RPG characters both have skills and **abilities** that are chosen ahead of time. However, only LARP characters need a costume and props, both of which you'll make or buy. Also, it's only in LARPing that you have to choose your character's **accent** and how they act!

A WHOLE NEW WORLD

STs create and run a LARP event by using props, costumes, buildings, **settings**, and even entire forests to create an imaginary world around you! Their goal is to make the people participating in their LARP feel immersed. This means they feel that they're really part of another world.

Every piece of these costumes was
chosen to add to the character's overall look.
There are all kinds of directions online
for how to make costume pieces!

Every LARP has guidelines about characters. These rules, which can be long or short, are often found on the LARP's website. If the LARP is based on something that already exists, like an RPG or book, there may also be sources you can read to help you get started creating a new character!

Choosing who you'll be in a LARP world doesn't just mean making a costume and props. You'll need to decide how your character acts—and then perform that way! Nobody but you decides what you do during the game. Throughout the game, you'll talk to player characters (PCs) like you and characters played by staff members, called nonplayer characters (NPCs).

IMMERSION

Immersion means that everyone stays in character to create the most **authentic** experience during a LARP. There are different levels of immersion in LARPing. A LARP with little immersion, for example, may allow phones. The rules of a LARP will explain exactly what you can and can't do when you're in character.

Some costumes can be hard to
wear all day in the sun. Make sure
to think ahead about the weather
before you choose a costume!

USING SKILLS

In LARP, you often have to announce
to those nearby when you use a skill.
For example, when a wizard casts, or
magically makes, a shooting fireball,
he shouts "Fireball! 15 damage!" to
the other players in battle. This lets
them know what hit them and how hard
it hit them.

Just like in the real world, characters have jobs and skills! In LARPing, you decide from a list of jobs—sometimes called classes or professions—specific to your LARP. What you choose places you within the imaginary society of the LARP. For example, you could choose to be a royal family member in a ruling class or a gunmaker in the soldier class.

Using special powers or objects is part of your character's set of skills. Being a knight, for example, means having sword-fighting skills. A wizard has skills in performing magic and spells. A soldier uses body strength and knowledge of different weapons to fight in battle.

Every LARP has different rules and ways of saying the effects of their weapons and skills during role-play.

CHOOSE A RACE

Since there are many different kinds of LARPS, making a character may mean choosing a race! Many fantasy LARPs are inspired by the works of J.R.R. Tolkien. A fantasy LARP may include humans, elves, and dwarves—or even different kinds of humans, elves, and dwarves! In his famous *Lord of the Rings* books, Tolkien made many races within these groups. He even invented new languages for his races!

Sci-fi LARPs can also have different races. Eclipse lets PCs choose their character type from a list of five human types and five **alien** races. Each has a certain look and set of skills.

COSTUMES CREATE CHARACTERS

Costume means only the clothing, makeup, and objects you wear. Your costume may be the most important thing you prepare for a LARP because it communicates to other LARPers who and what your character is and what you can do.

Some races in LARP must wear costumes
that cover their hands, feet, and face. Consider
how comfortable you want to be all day
before choosing a race to play!

PROPS

In LARPing, any props you carry that represent weapons, armor, tools, and even food and drink are physreps (FIHZ-rehps). "Physrep" is short for "physical representation," which means the prop looks like a real object in shape, color, and more. Costume and physreps can have more or less attention to exactness depending on the level of immersion set forth by the LARP.

Physreps can be made or found online. Foam swords, arrows, and bullets are made by Nerf and many other companies. The LARP's rules will say what kinds of weapons are allowed. This is usually based on the kind of role-play fighting in the LARP.

A boffer is a light weapon that's been padded with foam so people don't get hurt when it's used in battle. Always remember to pack your own physreps if there's going to be a battle!

BOFFER

ELVES, ELVES, ELVES

Elves and fairies were a part of ancient folktales from Norway. William Shakespeare's plays featured elves. Gary Gygax, the creator of D&D, was inspired by reading about Tolkien's elf races to include elves in his RPG. In a fantasy LARP, elves wear pointed earpieces as part of their costume.

STAYING IN CHARACTER

Even LARPers with acting experience can struggle with being in character all day for a LARP. It's not easy to make conversations up as you go! Try to think like your character. Decide ahead of time how your character walks, acts at meals, talks to friends, and deals with enemies. Remember what the rules say about how different races, classes, or creatures behave. Your character can be shy, brave, funny, or anything else you like within the ST's guidelines!

Practice being your character by joining as many activities as you can at your first few LARPs.

THE STORY NEEDS YOU

The STs want everyone at their LARP to have fun as a part of the story. Every small or large activity—like a meal or a battle—they've set up within the LARP is a chance for you to try new things. Let your character grow and change, just like the story!

Just like in real life, there's no way in LARP to know what you'll see, hear, and be a part of! Keep an open mind, observe everything around you, and jump right in if you think your character would be a part of an activity!

WEDDING PERFORMED DURING LARP

LET THE LARPING BEGIN!

By the time you arrive at a LARP, the STs will have set up props and furniture throughout the event space to create the LARP's imaginary setting. Since NPCs are played by staff, they're also usually on location ahead of time to help with setup. The LARP's website or rules should tell you exactly where to go when you arrive on location to check in.

Then, you'll get your costumes and physreps ready for the beginning of the event—sometimes there's even an opening **ceremony**! The game begins when the STs announce "lay on" or "game on." From then on, you'll have to stay in character!

HOW LONG?

When choosing a LARP, it's important to know in advance how long it'll last. Some are several hours long, while some of the most immersive events are a whole weekend, a week, or even 2 weeks! In those cases, players usually camp on location.

Some LARPs require a lot of running and moving, so don't forget to eat and drink plenty of water—especially on a hot day!

The wide range of STs makes LARPing a world with no limits. Each LARP comes from a different set of minds, with different goals and experiences that help them choose where to take their LARP. One day, maybe you'll be an ST and use your life experiences and interests to choose how a LARP will go!

Perhaps most importantly, LARPing can introduce you to new friends. Whether playing with old friends year after year at the same event or making new friends each time you play, you're sure to have treasured friendships and memories from LARPing!

LEARN FROM THE MASTERS!

If you're interested in becoming an ST, talk to other STs to learn from their experiences running LARPs. Also, talk to your LARP community. In LARP, you're surrounded by people from all sorts of fields—from writers to teachers to lawyers. Who knows what they can teach you!

LARP can introduce you to many talented people—and one day, even friends! For now, why not try out LARPing in your backyard with some friends?

29

GLOSSARY

ability: the power or skill to do something

accent: a way of saying words that is the same for people from a certain area

alien: a creature that comes from somewhere other than Earth

authentic: made the same way as the original, or shown to be true and trustworthy

ceremony: an event to honor or celebrate something

conversation: an informal talk involving two people or a small group of people

fantasy: having to do with a world produced in the imagination

participate: to take part in doing something with others

pirate: someone who attacks and steals from ships at sea

prop: an object used by a performer to create a desired effect in a scene on stage or in a movie

science fiction: stories about how people and societies are affected by imaginary science discoveries and inventions

setting: the rooms, painted backgrounds, furniture, and other objects used in a movie or play

wizard: a person who is skilled in magic or who has magical powers

FOR MORE INFORMATION

BOOKS

Blankenship, Lloyd, and Lane Boyd. *Woodworking for Young Makers: Fun and Easy Do-It-Yourself Projects.* San Francisco, CA: Maker Media, Inc., 2017.

Hart, Eric. *The Prop Building Guidebook: For Theatre, Film, and TV.* New York, NY: Routledge, 2017.

Thorsson, Shawn. *Props and Costume Armor: Create Realistic Science Fiction and Fantasy Weapons, Armor, and Accessories.* San Francisco, CA: Maker Media, Inc., 2016.

WEBSITES

How LARP Works
people.howstuffworks.com/larp1.htm
Read all about the experience of LARPing.

LARPing.org
larping.org/
Read about LARPs around the world, including youth-friendly events and organizations.

New to Prop and Costume Making?
punishedprops.com/new-maker/
This website is filled with directions, links, videos, and more.

INDEX